Achieving Financial Alignment

30 Biblical Principles for Ordering Your Financial Life

Published by
ABC Book Publishing

AbcBookPublishing.com
Printed in U.S.A.
Achieving Financial Alignment:

30 Biblical Principles for Ordering Your Financial Life

© Copyright 2008 by Richard A. Brott

ISBN: 1-60185-011-5
ISBN (EAN): 978-1-60185-011-9

i

About The Author

Rich Brott holds a Bachelor of Science degree in Business and Economics and a Master of Business Administration.

Rich has served in an executive position of some very successful businesses. He has functioned on the board of directors for churches, businesses, and charities and served on a college advisory board. Rich has traveled to more than 25 countries on teaching assignments and business concerns.

Rich Brott has authored over thirty-five books including:

- *5 Simple Keys to Financial Freedom*
- *10 Life-Changing Attitudes That Will Make You a Financial Success*
- *15 Biblical Responsibilities Leading to Financial Wisdom*
- *30 Biblical Principles for Managing Your Money*
- *35 Keys to Financial Independence*
- *A Biblical Perspective on Giving Generously*
- *A Biblical Perspective on Tithing & Giving*
- *A Biblical Perspective on Tithing Faithfully*
- *Achieving Financial Alignment*
- *Activating Your Personal Faith to Receive*
- *All the Financial Scriptures in the Bible*
- *Basic Principles for Business Success*
- *Basic Principles for Developing Personal and Business Vision*
- *Basic Principles for Managing a Successful Business*
- *Basic Principles for Maximizing Your Personal Cash Flow*
- *Basic Principles for Starting a Successful Business*

- *Basic Principles of Conservative Investing*
- *Biblical Principles for Achieving Personal Success*
- *Biblical Principles for Becoming Debt Free*
- *Biblical Principles for Building a Successful Business*
- *Biblical Principles for Financial Success - Student Workbook*
- *Biblical Principles for Financial Success - Teacher Workbook*
- *Biblical Principles for Personal Evangelism*
- *Biblical Principles for Releasing Financial Provision*
- *Biblical Principles for Staying Out of Debt*
- *Biblical Principles for Success in Personal Finance*
- *Biblical Principles That Create Success Through Productivity*
- *Business, Occupations, Professions & Vocations In the Bible*
- *Family Finance Handbook*
- *Family Finance Student Workbook*
- *Family Finance Teacher Workbook*
- *How to Receive Prosperity and Provision*
- *Prosperity Has a Purpose*
- *Public Relations for the Local Church*
- *Successful Time Management*

He and his wife Karen, have been married for 36 years. Rich Brott resides in Portland, Oregon, with his wife, three children, son-in-law and granddaughter.

Dedication

This book is dedicated to the greatest people in the world, my parents, William and Glenna Brott. The principles within this text were taught, lived and modeled throughout their lives.

Table of Contents

Achieving Financial Alignment:

30 Biblical Principles for Ordering Your Financial Life

Introduction

In the story of the feeding of the five thousand, Christ recognized the need of the crowd of people. Knowing that the people were hungry and should be fed, He took stock of the available resources. All they could find was a lad with five loaves and two fishes. So Christ used that. Through the miracle of multiplication, the entire multitude was fed. Instead of resting in the praise of the contented participants, Jesus was very concerned that nothing be wasted.

Have you ever wasted the blessing of God? What has God provided miraculously for you that you squandered? What income and finances has He given to you that you let slip away with frivolous spending?

Many people, deep in debt and lacking in self-discipline in their spending and contentment level, complain that their employers don't pay them enough, their taxes are much too high, their business costs have skyrocketed, or render some other excuse why they cannot plan for their financial future. Of course, some of these excuses may have a certain amount of legitimacy to them, but they don't excuse a person from the responsibility of making sure that they are not wasting any of the resources God has allowed to come through their hands.

The problem is rarely a lack of money; it is a lack of money management. Money management simply means self-management. Enjoy your journey to a re-aligning of your financial attitude and life!

Rich Brott

Principle 1

The Principle of ATTITUDE CONTROL

1 TIMOTHY 6:17
*Command those who are rich in this present world not to be arrogant
nor to put their hope in wealth, which is so uncertain.*

ℋere is a biblical principle that reminds us not
to think too highly of ourselves and our accomplishments.
The real truth of the matter is this: All that we have, all that
we are, and all good that comes to us is allowed by God. If
you cannot walk in humility now, what are the chances of
that happening after you have been supernaturally blessed?

When we look upon the attitudes and heart of a
blessed person, what will we discover? What is the heart
like? What kind of attitude does one need to receive the
blessing? What about the heart of a blessed person? What
theme was so important to Jesus that He talked about it more
than anything else? Was it heaven? Was it repentance? Was
it prayer? Was it salvation? No. It was the subject of money.
He knew that if He had our money, He would certainly have
our hearts.

11

What about the attitude of a blessed person? Overall, the principal attitude must be that all money and all possessions belong to God. He trusts us with the care of these things until we prove ourselves unworthy of His trust. It is not our money, so it's not our problem to worry about. It is our basic responsibility as good stewards to use it correctly, decisions that are the result of a proper attitude.

Principle 2

The Principle of
BEING A FAITHFUL STEWARD

1 CORINTHIANS 4:2–3
Now it is required that those who have been given a trust must prove faithful.

A steward is not an owner, but a manager. God is always the owner, and we are always the managers of the many and various stewardships He has given to us. But in order to fulfill this role He has given to us as extenders of His grace, we need to know all the areas of stewardship for which we are accountable.

The areas of good stewardship that He requires of us are almost limitless. They would of course include life itself, the gift of children, and the stewardship of His creation. Additionally, we would include the stewardship of our communication, the stewardship of time, the stewardship of truth, and the stewardship of talents or giftings. Discovering and developing our spiritual gifts and natural talents for the purpose of blessing others and glorifying God is our duty.

Nearly two-thirds of the parables of Jesus deal with stewardship, or the proper use of money. In the New Testament there are thirty-eight parables, twelve of which are about money. One out of every six verses in Matthew, Mark, and Luke has to do with money and individual fiduciary responsibility. As stewards, it is our responsibility to trust God to supply our needs. We have been given responsibility over the natural resources of the earth according to Genesis 1:28.

Matthew 10:8 instructs us that as we have abundantly received, we are to freely give.

The account of the rich young ruler in Mark 10:17-22 tells the story of a man and all his possessions. He thought what he possessed belonged only to him. This story was not a lesson on tithing and giving, rather one on stewardship. When the Ten Commandments were mentioned by Jesus, the response from the wealthy young ruler was that he had honored those in his life from a very young age.

If the Lord had asked him about whether or not he was a tither, most likely the wealthy young ruler would have also replied in the affirmative. Next Jesus hones in on the real problem...the man's possessions. Jesus wanted to confront him concerning his priorities, his stewardship, and where the real ownership of these things lay. But this was just too hard for the rich young ruler. He had to leave with a countenance full of dismay and a sad heart. The rich young ruler did not understand that the possessions he had been entrusted with had been given to him for a purpose. That purpose was to include sharing his wealth with the poor and needy of the earth.

Since stewards are charged with great authority and responsibility, their character cannot be flawed. Good stewards of time and finance are not only faithful and responsible; there is an honesty and integrity about them. In Webster's the word integrity is defined as "being complete, unimpaired, perfect condition, of sound moral principle, uprightness." Proverbs 19:1 says, "Better is the poor that walketh in his integrity, than he that is perverse in his lips, and is a fool." True riches are not determined by what a person possesses, but by the integrity of what he is.

God is interested in our willingness to manage and administrate all that He has given to us. In this sense, we could say that Jesus Christ is to be given complete freedom and lordship over our entire life. Like every other area of stewardship, God is interested in the whole picture, not just a part or a percentage.

The servants (stewards) in Bible times who were entrusted with a portion of the master's possessions were challenged not only to keep them, but to utilize them and multiply the property.

LUKE 16:1–8
Jesus told His disciples: "There was a rich man whose manager was accused of wasting his possessions. So he called him in and asked him, 'What is this I hear about you? Give an account of your management, because you cannot be manager any longer.' The manager said to himself, 'What shall I do now? My master is taking away my job. I'm not strong enough to dig, and I'm ashamed to beg—I know what I'll do so that, when I lose my job here, people will welcome me into their houses.' So he called in each one of his master's debtors. He asked the first, 'How much do you owe my master?' 'Eight hundred gallons of olive oil,' he replied. The manager told him, 'Take your bill, sit down quickly, and make it four hundred.' Then he asked the second, 'And how much do you owe?' 'A thousand bushels of wheat,' he replied. He told him, 'Take your bill and

make it eight hundred.' The master commended the dishonest manager because he had acted shrewdly. For the people of this world are more shrewd in dealing with their own kind than are the people of the light."

The rich man's steward of Luke 16 was not dependable and apparently did not fulfill his financial responsibilities to his lord. He was about to lose his position because he had violated his fiduciary relationship to the master of the house.

The steward's lord commended him because he finally showed some ingenuity and ambition, even though it was for his own personal gain and benefit. The steward is not commended because he showed good fiduciary sensitivity, rather because he had done wisely for himself.

The steward who was about to be dismissed made every attempt to better his cause through any means available, even though that cause was self-serving. The shrewdness with which the unjust servant negated his fiduciary responsibility to his lord was commended. He promoted his cause with the utmost care and effort. With an unprincipled passion, he sought to use his master's money in securing advantage after his inevitable dismissal. Christ was simply asking those to whom He spoke to be as inventive for a much better cause.

Principle 3

The Principle of BEING PROACTIVE

MATTHEW 17:27
"Go to the lake and throw out your line. Take the first fish you catch;
open its mouth."

$\mathcal{W}$e are to take action—to be proactive. The abilities and giftings He provides motivate us to action. Sometimes it takes our persistence in doing the same things faithfully with the heart of a servant. Other times it is useful to try new things or new methods and seek after new opportunities. Sometimes it is the steady plodding that brings the success of the blessed life.

Ecclesiastes 9:11 says, "The race is not to the swift or the battle to the strong, nor does food come to the wise or wealth to the brilliant or favor to the learned; but time and chance happen to them all." Hebrews 12:1-2 advises, "Let us throw off everything that hinders and the sin that so easily entangles, and let us run with perseverance the race marked out for us. Let us fix our eyes on Jesus, the author and perfecter of our faith."

Proverbs 21:5 instructs us that, "Steady plodding brings prosperity; hasty speculation brings poverty" (RSV).

Sometimes being proactive means stepping up our faith giving. You certainly cannot out give God! Taking action, being proactive, and not giving up are principles for living the life of a blessed person.

Nothing will be thrown into our laps. No, financial prosperity is not an unconditional providential blessing, and yes, conditions are attached. We are to take action and be proactive. The abilities and giftings God provides motivate us to action. Sometimes it takes our persistence in doing the same things faithfully with the heart of a servant. Other times it is time to try new things, new methods, and seek new opportunities. Sometimes the steady plodding brings the success of the blessed life.

God allows us to possess certain things, but mere possession is not ownership. Those things you possess can be taken from you in an instant. The scores of dishonest accounting firms and corrupt corporate CEOs of our day have seen to that. Billions of honest dollars invested by millions of wage earners have disappeared. Wage earners have seen their retirement savings disappear in a matter of mere months. You can possess, but it is God who owns. You may earn a living, but it is God who gives to you the ability to earn. God is the one who gives to you the power to get wealth.

Let's note what Scripture says about just how much you really own.

DEUTERONOMY 8:18
But remember the LORD your God, for it is he who gives you the ability to produce wealth.

PSALM 24:1
The earth is the LORD'S, and everything in it, the world, and all who live in it.

PSALM 50:10–11
For every animal of the forest is mine, and the cattle on a thousand hills. I know every bird in the mountains, and the creatures of the field are mine.

PSALM 100:3
Know that the LORD is God. It is he who made us, and we are his; we are his people, the sheep of his pasture.

EZEKIEL 18:4
For every living soul belongs to me.

HAGGAI 2:8
"The silver is mine and the gold is mine," declares the LORD Almighty.

ACTS 17:28
For in him we live and move and have our being.

ROMANS 12:1
Therefore, I urge you, brothers, in view of God's mercy, to offer your bodies as living sacrifices, holy and pleasing to God.

ECCLESIASTES 9:11
The race is not to the swift or the battle to the strong, nor does food come to the wise or wealth to the brilliant or favor to the learned; but time and chance happen to them all.

HEBREWS 12:1–2

This verse tells us what to do and what to avoid:

Let us throw off everything that hinders and the sin that so easily entangles, and let us run with perseverance the race marked out for us. Let us fix our eyes on Jesus, the author and perfecter of our faith.

Being a person of principle requires hard work, diligence, and proactivity. Nothing will be handed to you without these requirements. The Bible says that if a person does not work, he should not eat. Now that's a pretty simple yet direct statement. Does God want to bless us supernaturally? Of course He does. Will His blessing come to us if we are lazy, idle, slothful, passive, and unwilling to roll up our sleeves and get to work? No, I don't believe so.

PROVERBS 21:5
Steady plodding brings prosperity; hasty speculation brings poverty. (RSV).

PROVERBS 21:25–26
The sluggard's craving will be the death of him, because his hands refuse to work. All day long he craves for more, but the righteous give without sparing.

Taking action, being proactive, not giving up—all are principles for living the life of a blessed person.

Principle 4

The Principle of BEING SATISFIED

1 TIMOTHY 6:8
But if we have food and clothing, we will be content with that.

*M*illions of people today are striving to accumulate possessions and wealth. It is hard to be satisfied with what we have when the world's entire system is geared toward making us unhappy with everything we have and desirous of everything we don't have. We face a discontented culture. The question is: How much money does it take to be content? Usually just a little bit more. That's the problem—money cannot buy contentment or happiness. We must work toward contentment and contend for happiness.

> "Contentment is a pearl of great price, and whoever procures it at the expense of ten thousand desires makes a wise and a happy purchase." —John Balguy

Making money is certainly not wrong, as long as it doesn't violate the laws of our land or God's Word. The all-for-me and none-for-others way of man's thinking is immoral. People who follow God's principles will be good stewards if they obey the law of giving.

They will find happiness in exact proportion to the degree in which they give. They will be content with life and what they have been given.

Money and happiness are not mutually exclusive. Benjamin Franklin noted, "Money never made a man happy yet, nor will it. There is nothing in its nature to produce happiness. The more a man has, the more he wants. Instead of filling a vacuum, it makes one." He also said, "Contentment makes poor men rich; discontentment makes rich men poor."

Being a good steward begins with the blessing of God, but the test and fruit of good stewardship is how we use those blessings. Are we a conduit or do we stop the stream of God's favor. Do we allow the river to flow, or do we dam up God's supply? To me it is a matter of management, not ownership. Are we to give only a little and hoard the rest for our own pleasure? I think not. God expects us to use what we need (He has promised to supply our need), then to multiply and return the rest. Stewardship is trust, knowing and disbursing His blessing. The blessing of stewardship is in giving.

Many wealthy people wish they had friends. Some of the most prominent people in the world are some of the saddest people on earth. Even their money cannot hide their unhappiness and displeasure with life. It is sad when people spend an entire lifetime trying to get rich, only to find that when they finally become rich, they are still unhappy, still dissatisfied with life, and still sad.

Jesus let us know in Luke 12:15 that a person's life and happiness do not consist of things, possessions, and money. In other words, all the possessions in the world will not bring contentment, nor will they buy happiness.

The rich man in Luke 12:19 declared that after working hard for many years, accumulating great wealth and all the goods the world could offer him, he could now be free to take it easy by eating, drinking or being merry. He had dedicated his whole life to accumulating great possessions for such a time as this. Jesus called this man a fool because of his thinking. His thinking was wrong, his priorities were wrong, and because of wrong thinking, he was unable to be the kind of good steward he was required to be.

The Christian is not to love money. He is to love God. The Scriptures are not so much concerned about our having wealth, but are concerned with how it is obtained and how it is managed. God allows us to be partners with Him. God's role in the partnership is to meet our needs (Philippians 4:19). Our role in the partnership is to work (2 Thessalonians 3:10). Our work is a means of worship and ministry. When we work, we meet the needs of our family and serve the Lord at the same time. We are also to work with proper motives (Colossians 3:23-24).

The rich man, whom Jesus called a fool, was an example of a person who loved money more than life itself. But God had other plans for him. After being called a fool and after working selfishly for a lifetime just so he could retire in pleasure and ease, God said that tonight was his last evening on earth.

Harmful Desires

1 TIMOTHY 6:9
People who want to get rich fall into temptation and a trap and into many foolish and harmful desires that plunge men into ruin and destruction.

Not Loving Money

1 TIMOTHY 6:10
For the love of money is a root of all kinds of evil. Some people, eager for money, have wandered from the faith and pierced themselves with many griefs.

All About Greed

LUKE 12:16–18
"The ground of a certain rich man produced a good crop. He thought to himself, 'What shall I do? I have no place to store my crops.' Then he said, 'This is what I'll do. I will tear down my barns and build bigger ones, and there I will store all my grain and my goods.'"

1 TIMOTHY 6:6
"Now godliness with contentment is great gain."

In this passage Jesus is telling us that we should find contentment in what we have instead of living in the discontent of what we do not have. We are to be grateful for what we have been blessed with and stop always striving for more.

GENESIS 2:15–16
The LORD God placed the man in the Garden of Eden as its gardener, to tend and care for it. But the LORD God gave the man this warning: "You may eat any fruit in the garden except fruit from the Tree of Conscience—for its fruit will open your eyes to make you aware of right and wrong, good and bad. If you eat its fruit, you will be doomed to die."

GENESIS 3:1–6

The serpent was the craftiest of all the creatures the LORD God had made. So the serpent came to the woman. "Really?" he asked. "None of the fruit in the garden? God says you mustn't eat any of it?" "Of course we may eat it," the woman told him. "It's only the fruit from the tree at the center of the garden that we are not to eat. God says we mustn't eat it or even touch it, or we will die." "That's a lie!" the serpent hissed. "You'll not die! God knows very well that the instant you eat it you will become like him, for your eyes will be opened—you will be able to distinguish good from evil!" The woman was convinced. How lovely and fresh looking it was! And it would make her so wise! So she ate some of the fruit and gave some to her husband, and he ate it too.

GENESIS 3:23

So the LORD God banished him forever from the Garden of Eden, and sent him out to farm the ground from which he had been taken. (RSV)

Very little commentary is needed here. Adam and Eve had the privilege of living in a garden so beautiful that it was nearly indescribable. They could enjoy its beauty and bask in its atmosphere and eat of its fruit, save one tree. Yet they were not content and sought to have everything, when they actually needed nothing else. The result was personally devastating to them.

Principle 5

The Principle of
CARING FOR OUR POSSESSIONS

1 TIMOTHY 6:20
Timothy, guard what has been entrusted to your care.

MATTHEW 19:21
"If you want to give it all you've got," Jesus replied, "go sell your possessions; give everything to the poor. All your wealth will then be in heaven. Then come follow me." (THE MESSAGE)

*B*ecause we are not our own, we should dedicate to God all that we are, all that we own, and all that we will ever be. You are God's, so all you have belongs to God. You simply manage your possessions for Him. Your business belongs to God. When everything you have belongs to God, it takes off all the pressure.

In many countries, citizens pride themselves on private property ownership. In reality, all property, possessions, money, and wealth belong to God. We are simply managers of what belongs to Him. All the land and all property still belong to the Creator.

How do you care for those possessions God has entrusted to you? Do your keep your house in good repair both outside and inside? Is your house clean and spotless? Do you organize and keep your yard equipment and tools in a safe dry place, or do you leave them lying around in the rain to rust?

Do you keep the oil and fluids fresh in your car, or do you let it go for several thousand miles before you drain and refill? Are your vehicles kept clean on the inside and outside? You see, good stewardship involves more than just having possessions and material goods; it goes to the core of how you care for them. You are caring for God's blessing. If you don't care how you treat the blessings God has allowed you to receive, how can you expect to keep them, let alone ask for more?

God is a good caretaker. He is very organized. He created and continues to manage galaxies, the universe, billions of stars, the sun, moon, and earth. He maintains His creation very well. We are to be equally as good at the organization and management of our affairs. Everything we have belongs to the Lord.

Principle 6

The Principle of CONTEMPLATION

2 TIMOTHY 2:7
Reflect on what I am saying, for the Lord will give you insight into all this.

How ow often do you take the time to reflect upon your financial responsibilities and stewardship obligations? Your stewardship defines your relationship with the Lord. How you manage what God has entrusted to you is an accurate reflection of your heart. Does your heart reflect a good understanding that everything you are and everything you have are nothing more than stewardship gifts from heaven? We are nothing more than managers of God's good gifts.

What is your relationship to God? Do you have a good personal relationship with Him? Do you spend time developing this relationship? A good relationship is built upon trust. A good relationship is built upon faith, confidence, and expectation. God expects you to do a good job taking care of your gifts: gifts of talent, time, health, possessions, and wealth. Many things come and go in our life, but gifts given by God are with us virtually every minute of every day. Having said that, our daily decisions and daily walk should reflect the trust relationship we have developed with God, and this relationship should be growing closer and maturing continually.

God places a lot of trust in us; it is more than just money and finances. Our entire being and how we handle faithfulness, responsibility, accountability, honesty, and integrity are involved. Stewardship is bringing everything we have to offer under the Lordship of Christ. What kind of a person makes a good steward? A person who has great respect for God and His creation. Are you a good steward?

Is your relationship with God reflected in every financial decision you make? When you receive income from the job God has blessed you with, do you pause to reflect on His goodness before you do anything else, or do you quickly spend it on nonessentials without regard to making the wise money-management decisions you know you should be making? Do you mirror the image of God? Do you reflect the wisdom of God in your financial life? Are you replicating His will in your financial world? Are you seeking insight and understanding before you initiate what seems right in your own eyes?

2 CORINTHIANS 3:18
But we Christians have no veil over our faces; we can be mirrors that brightly reflect the glory of the Lord. And as the Spirit of the Lord works within us, we become more and more like him. (RSV)

Principle 7

The Principle of CORRECT GIVING

MATTHEW 6:2
"So when you give to the needy, do not announce it with trumpets, as the hypocrites do in the synagogues and on the streets, to be honored by men. I tell you the truth, they have received their reward in full."

$\mathcal{G}$iving to the needy is an essential Christian value and responsibility. We are instructed to do so. Doing so regularly is like giving to the Lord. You may think that you are poor, but you can always find someone poorer than yourself.

A few years ago I was in Mexico for a series of meetings, and I stayed with a very poor Mexican family. This family lived in a very simple apartment, with very modest furnishings. They had no transportation and relied solely upon the city bus system to get them around. They walked to their place of employment. During the week that I was with them, I noticed that twice during the week someone came in and cleaned their apartment for them. This seemed very odd to me as I have yet to have someone outside my family clean my own house. Upon inquiry, my host family told me that they hire another family each week to come in and clean their apartment because they wanted to help the poor in their city. This family had very little to live on and every bit of income, no matter how small, was very helpful to them.

Growing up as a preacher's kid, I remember one very proud man in my father's church. He didn't seem to have much money, though he dressed well, wore bold fashionable rings on his fingers, and always flashed large rolls of currency in his pockets. He was always one of the first to give when needs of the church were presented. But he usually did so with a loud voice and made sure everyone in the church knew that he was giving and how much he was giving. He seemed to have a need for everyone to know. Perhaps he was receiving his reward instantly. It is charitable to give, but be careful about the manner in which it is done.

Principle 8

The Principle of EQUAL GIVING

2 CORINTHIANS 8:10–12

And here is my advice about what is best for you in this matter: Last year you were the first not only to give but also to have the desire to do so. Now finish the work, so that your eager willingness to do it may be matched by your completion of it, according to your means. For if the willingness is there, the gift is acceptable according to what one has, not according to what he does not have.

Equal giving does not equate to equal sacrifice. Our lifestyle of stewardship must reflect not only generous giving, but also sacrificial giving. When we are quick to acknowledge that all of our money and possessions come from a loving God, our role as a sacrificial giver is made much easier.

The principle of equal giving directs us to assess and examine how we manage our finances so that we can give to Him according to how God has blessed us. It enables us to rethink our lifestyle and to reorder the priorities in our life. In doing so, we will reallocate our gifts and resources to the work of God. We will give "over and above."

Principle 9

The Principle of FIRST THINGS NOW

*T*he biblical principle of first things now is all about proper perspective and proper motives. It is about doing the right thing now, getting your priorities in proper alignment. If your sole purpose in life is to make money and accumulate stuff for yourself, then you are already headed down the wrong path. Jesus said the kingdom of God is to be sought first. This does not mean to seek first for a while and then to switch to a second goal of accumulating vast amounts of material possessions second. It just means that our focus must always be on kingdom matters and kingdom priorities. As we keep our priorities in line, the things we need will be provided.

Jesus knew that men and women would have trouble keeping their hearts focused on their real purpose for being here. That's why, in the Sermon on the Mount, He said:

MATTHEW 6:19–21
"Do not store up for yourselves treasures on earth, where moth and rust destroy, and where thieves break in and steal. But store up for yourselves treasures in heaven, where moth and rust do not destroy, and where thieves do not break in and steal. For where your treasure is, there your heart will be also."

MATTHEW 6:33
"But seek first his kingdom and his righteousness, and all these things will be given to you as well."

Putting God first in our lives alleviates us from the task of having to worry about everything else. Seeking His kingdom and righteousness first is simply making God the priority in our lives. Verse 33 outlines for us a priority, a principle, and a promise. Our priority is to seek God's will and way first. The principle is to focus on kingdom activity. The promise is that when we seek Him first and focus on the business of the kingdom, God will take care of all our other needs.

There is always the temptation to put our money first. Do you remember the rich young ruler who came to Jesus and said he wanted to follow Christ? How Jesus responded to Him didn't make him very happy. Jesus told him to give his money away and follow Him. You see, it wasn't the money that was wrong; it was that this young man placed his money ahead of and above all else.

> **"When wealth is lost, nothing is lost; when health is lost, something is lost; when character is lost, all is lost."**
> **—Billy Graham**

If we have too much money, there is always the danger that we can depend upon it ultimately. Does your life reveal your desire to put God first? The Lord admonishes us to seek first His kingdom, His way of doing things, and not to worry about possessions. Acquisition of possessions never satisfies. We only want more and more. That is why our focus must be on needs, not wants.

What do we need? Generally that would include food and water, sunshine and air, rain and shelter. Beyond these basic survival needs could come the need for friends, family, relationships, self-esteem, etc. What we don't need is more things. Materialism is a focus on things of matter rather than on the things of God. Before we put all our time, energy, interests, and life into what we deem valuable, Jesus is telling us to stop and get our focus on things of eternal value.

Moses considered reproach for Christ as greater riches than all the treasures in Egypt.

> HEBREWS 11:26
> *He regarded disgrace for the sake of Christ as of greater value than the treasures of Egypt, because he was looking ahead to his reward.*

The biblical mandate is to seek first the things of the kingdom. The lives of believers are spoiled if they are completely wrapped up in possessions and absorbed in the pursuit of material accumulation. We must ask God to help us develop an attitude of serving Him faithfully and a life that is free of materialism so we can pursue the extension of kingdom priorities instead of human wants. After all, our whole purpose in life is to give to others, share with others, and bless others just as we have been blessed.

Personal prosperity will never come at the expense of ethical values and biblical principles. Settle it once and for all in your heart and mind. God values obedience and makes it a condition of His blessing. Until your personal life and financial life get in line with His morality and commandments, don't expect financial miracles to be the norm in your life. Those who have not learned this lesson often struggle for years with the burden of heavy debt.

An interesting group of Scriptures surround the story of rebuilding the ancient temple. The main characters in this story are Joshua the high priest, Zerubbabel the governor of Judah, Haggai the prophet, and the Israelites. It seems they had become so involved in their own personal lives and building their own houses that they had neglected the building, finishing, and operational needs of God's house.

God apparently finally had His fill of the people's inability to focus upon the principle of "first things now," and He sent word to the governor through Haggai the prophet. The message to be delivered was straightforward, direct, to the point, and quite harsh. He stated their current condition, summarized the problem, and stated the result. There is nothing ambiguous about the mind of God.

> HAGGAI 1:5–10
> Look at the result: You plant much but harvest little. You have scarcely enough to eat or drink and not enough clothes to keep you warm. Your income disappears, as though you were putting it into pockets filled with holes! "Think it over," says the LORD Almighty. "Consider how you have acted and what has happened as a result! Then go up into the mountains, bring down timber, and rebuild my Temple, and I will be pleased with it and appear there in my glory," says the LORD. "You hope for much but get so little. And when you bring it home, I blow it away—it doesn't last at all. Why? Because my Temple lies in ruins, and you don't care. Your only concern is your own fine homes. That is why I am holding back the rains from heaven and giving you such scant crops." (RSV)

What are you doing in your personal financial life that is not pleasing to God? Why are you out of the flow of God's divine blessing? How many problems have you brought into your life because you have failed to line up with the principles of God's Word? Don't you think it's time for you to assess your current lifestyle and make the proper adjustments needed to bring your life back in line? It's never too late to begin again. God is awesome and full of mercy. But He does want your priorities to be in line with the Word. Get your financial priorities straight, and watch the blessings of heaven begin to flow in your direction.

Principle 10

The Principle of
FREEDOM FROM THE LOVE OF MONEY

HEBREWS 13:4–5
Keep your lives free from the love of money and be content with what you have, because God has said.

*H*ow hard is it to keep our head straight, our heart pure, and our body clean? This verse admonishes us to be careful and be content. Be careful that you seek God and not things. Be careful that as you are blessed with money you don't begin to fall in love with it.

One of the most noted pastors in the history of the Christian church was Charles Spurgeon. He was an English fundamentalist Baptist minister. After pastoring Metropolitan Tabernacle in London for some thirty-eight years, he died at the age of fifty-seven. Since his death, collections of his various writings, including sermons and commentaries, have been published in many different forms.

From his "The Scales of Judgment," he says this: "It is no easy thing to stand the trial of prosperity." On yet another occasion (Sunday sermon on May 13, 1855), he said, "Continued worldly prosperity is a fiery trial."

1 CORINTHIANS 10:11–12
Don't be so naive and self-confident. You're not exempt. You could fall flat on your face as easily as anyone else. Forget about self-confidence; it's useless. Cultivate God-confidence. (THE MESSAGE)

Principle 11

The Principle of GIVING THE TENTH

GENESIS 14:20
Then Abram gave him a tenth of everything.

Abraham tithed the tenth before any other commitment was made. Jacob paid a tithe. Joseph instructed the people to prepare for years of famine by tithing 20 percent on their current abundance of harvest. Zaccheus gave one half of all his money. Barnabas gave a parcel of land. The widow gave all that she had. Whatever we give, either the tenth or beyond the tenth, should be given from the start, off the top, before we commit to anything else. Proverbs 3:9 directs us to honor the Lord from our wealth by giving the first of all our produce. The Jews were told to dedicate the firstborn son and the firstborn beast to God. It was all to be given from the top.

Principle 12

The Principle of GOD IS MY MASTER

MATTHEW 6:24
"No one can serve two masters. Either he will hate the one and love the other, or he will be devoted to the one and despise the other. You cannot serve both God and Money."

Stewardship is the management of our entire life—all that we have, all that we are. We are commanded, as believers, to obey God in the area of giving tithes and offerings. God doesn't need our money. He is not broke. What He wants is us. His goal is relational, not financial. Stewardship is more than money. Stewardship is more than our talents, our giving, our tithing, and our money. Stewardship is the management of our entire life for the purpose of glorifying and magnifying God. Our life management is a reflection of our relationship with Him. Who has become your master?

Principle 13

The Principle of GOOD INTENTIONS

$\mathcal{G}$od is interested in your motives. Can you be trusted with prosperity? If you cannot be trusted now in poverty, why should you be given prosperity? Jesus said in Matthew 6:33, "But seek ye first the kingdom of God, and his righteousness; and all these things shall be added unto you" (KJV). How much money, health, wealth, position, prominence, and influence can God trust you to handle? Have you been 100 percent trustworthy in the past with all that God has given to you? If not, why should He give you more?

Do you give a full day's work to your employer for a fair wage in return? If not, why should He trust you with a better job? Are you a good steward with the wage He has given to you? Are you judicious about how you spend your earnings? If not, why should you be trusted with a higher rate of pay if you are not a good financial manager with what you have already been given? Do you maintain your car, truck, home, etc., now? If you cannot be responsible now for taking care of the possessions God has already given you, why should He bless you with more?

47

If God were to look down upon you with the idea of blessing you beyond your expectations, but first checked your money motive, what would He find? Would you be the one He could trust with great wealth, knowing that you would use it to bless the kingdom of God? Or would you be the one who simply used it to gain more personal possessions and to live a life of personal fulfillment and easy living? The focus of many people is pleasure, sensual indulgence, money, selfishness, power, and flattery. People who live this way do nothing of lasting or eternal value. They have no ultimate purpose in mind. As Christians, we need to have eternal values and purpose in mind.

Our motives and priorities must be for God and His kingdom first, ourselves last. Sometimes we get jealous of the success of others who are not Christian. They seem to be happy and rich and enjoying a life of luxury. A musician and prophet in Old Testament times by the name of Asaph said, "I was envious at the foolish, when I saw the prosperity of the wicked" (Psalm 73:3).

Ungodly men and women may achieve material prosperity apart from God, but they can never achieve the deep-settled peace that comes from God. Riches gained without God are a snare and do not bring peace. Prosperity that comes from God brings, not only an abundance of possessions, but also emotional peace, happiness, and great joy.

Do you know why some wicked people are rich today? The Bible provides a simple explanation: The wicked who are rich are simply holding the wealth that God someday will give His children. "And the wealth of the sinner is laid up for the righteous" (Proverbs 13:22, ASV).

In the Old Testament, Solomon tells us in Proverbs 22:7 that the borrower is a servant to the lender. In the New Testament, Luke 16:13 says, "No servant can serve two masters. Either he will hate the one and love the other, or he will be devoted to the one and despise the other. You cannot serve both God and money." Both Scripture passages confirm each other. How can you properly serve God when you are a slave or servant to a creditor? When you want to follow God wholeheartedly but are a slave to materialism, a conflict of interest arises. You need to be free of discontentment to follow the will of God for your life.

Your heart concerning the kingdom of God may be proper and principled, but if your motives and decisions are influenced at all by a love for money or the things money can buy, your thinking is tarnished. If your thinking remains tainted, it won't be long until your heart is also corrupted.

Principle 14

❋ ❦ ❋

The Principle of HARMFUL DESIRES

1 TIMOTHY 6:9–10
People who want to get rich fall into temptation and a trap and into many foolish and harmful desires that plunge men into ruin and destruction.

$\mathcal{I}$ am always wary of people who openly tell others that they have an intense desire to become rich. If they are engaging their thinking during this statement, they will add the disclaimer at some point in the conversation that their desire to become wealthy is to be able to give more to charity. Not that there is anything wrong with riches or being wealthy, but too many people seek after it insincerely. They resist education, hard work, and productivity. They seek to become rich via an inheritance or the lottery. God's way is by becoming a generous giver right now regardless of your current income and by forward thinking, personal ingenuity, and person productivity.

Great assets and possessions do not guarantee a long, full life, nor one filled with happiness and security. Your value is not in what you have or what you own. Your value and personal fulfillment is in what you are or what you strive to become. Your riches on this earth have no relationship to the riches you send before you to inherit in the life to come.

MATTHEW 19:23–24
As he watched him go, Jesus told his disciples, "Do you have any idea how difficult it is for the rich to enter God's kingdom? Let me tell you, it's easier to gallop a camel through a needle's eye than for the rich to enter God's kingdom." (THE MESSAGE)

Be very careful of what you seek to obtain in this life. Be careful of harmful desires that could lead you to personal ruin. Your trust should be only in the Lord Jesus Christ and not in the things of this world. He is your source of true wealth. Riches come and go. Wealth comes and goes. Jobs are here one day and gone the next. I have friends who have lived in seemingly great wealth, only to be living in poverty the next year. Our accumulated wealth, our position in a company, our status in life, our health, etc., can all change very quickly. Life storms rise without warning. The winds of change threaten our normal existence. Accidents happen, diseases appear, and upheaval brings change to our expectations.

ECCLESIASTES 2:24–26
So I decided that there was nothing better for a man to do than to enjoy his food and drink and his job. Then I realized that even this pleasure is from the hand of God. For who can eat or enjoy apart from him? For God gives those who please him wisdom, knowledge, and joy; but if a sinner becomes wealthy, God takes the wealth away from him and gives it to those who please him. So here, too, we see an example of foolishly chasing the wind. (RSV)

Be careful of what you desire. Temptation is very real; many are unable to resist the pleasures that wealth and prosperity can bring.

Principle 15

The Principle of HEART CHOICES

2 CORINTHIANS 9:7
Each man should give what he has decided in his heart to give, not reluctantly or under compulsion.

*T*he decision of how much to give is always left up to us. Of course we know the principle of the tenth that always belongs to God. But giving is more of an attitude than an amount. Get the heart and attitude right, and the amount will be exactly as it is supposed to be. God doesn't want us to give without thinking, nor does He want our leftovers. He desires that we give out of our best resources, our firstfruits, and lay our best gifts upon the altar of giving.

Our giving starts with our tithing. But it does not relieve us of our responsibility to meet other needs as they become known. When you give, give as though you are giving to God. With that attitude adjustment, you don't have to worry about it becoming routine, as in simply paying a financial obligation. When you pay the monthly mortgage or the utility bills, you are giving under compulsion—you are not given a choice. The Scripture says to simply give as you feel in your heart, not reluctantly or under compulsion.

Make your giving an act of worship! Give because He is worthy to receive. Give because you want to give. Give because you enjoy giving. Give because you have received. Give because you have been blessed. Give because your family is blessed. Give because you want to honor your Creator!

Principle 16

The Principle of **HONESTY IN OUR GIVING**

MALACHI 3:8, 10
"Will a man rob God? Yet you rob me. But you ask, 'How do we rob you?' In tithes and offerings. Bring the whole tithe into the storehouse, that there may be food in My house. Test me in this,' says the LORD Almighty, 'and see if I will not throw open the flood gates of heaven and pour out so much blessing that you will not have room enough for it.'"

Three things stand out in this reference. The first is the word rob. In no uncertain terms, this Scripture says that, yes, we can rob God by withholding what is rightfully His. Second is the challenge to test God. The Christian walk is designed to be a walk of faith. If our heart is right, we can take God at His Word. What He says will happen. Finally is the blessing. God has promised that He will open heaven's storehouse and flood us with His abundance.

Billy Graham once said, "You cannot get around it, the Scriptures promise material and spiritual benefits to the man who gives to God. You cannot out give God. I challenge you to try it and see."

How much should we give? No one can tell you for sure, but if you are not giving God His tenth, that is a place to begin. You must begin to give regularly a percentage of your paycheck, your bonuses, your increases, etc.

Malachi 3:8 refers to tithes and offerings. This means returning 10 percent of what belongs to God without question, plus offerings. He has placed in our hands the opportunity to decide how much our offerings should be. Just make sure that you give to God first. By doing so, you will never have to worry about having your needs met.

Principle 17

The Principle of
LIVING A DISCIPLINED LIFE

$\mathcal{I}$f we are to lead prosperous and successful lives (prosperity is not to be thought of as just having money), we have to apply biblical instruction to work hard and lead a disciplined life. Clearly, we are to do the very best we possibly can with the talents and strengths God has given us. A lot of people think that the world (that just means you and me) owes them a living. This kind of attitude destroys the work ethic in our society. Our country's welfare system does little to build character and establish the needy into better life-changing environments. To give money year after year to those who are idle and not expect any change in lifestyle does little to improve society for future generations.

Although Jesus said, "Ye have the poor always with you" (Matthew 26:11, KJV), the Western world has been blessed beyond measure. Those we consider poor by our country's standards could be considered rich by the measurements of the entire world. How many families in our society are without a television set or two or three? How many in this country do not have access to transportation? How many do not have shelter when they want it? How many do not enjoy the basics of life? Yes, we are a very blessed people.

Living a responsible and disciplined life requires financial discipline. Larry Burkett, a Christian economist who went to meet his heavenly reward in 2003, once noted that in 1929 the majority of all home purchases were made in cash. Roughly 95 percent of purchase transactions were paid in cash. Today only 5 percent of homes are purchased with cash, and 95 percent are mortgaged.

In the years prior to 1945, almost no cars were financed. It was almost unthinkable to purchase a vehicle with loaned money. If you didn't have the cash, you didn't purchase a car. Yet by contrast today, the average person has seven credit cards, at least one financed vehicle, and a mortgaged home loan. Credit card debt is at an all time high; nearly 72 percent of people never pay off their credit card balances each month. Where is the financial discipline of people today? It seems it doesn't exist.

It is sad when Christ has called us to be free people, yet many become enslaved to debt.

GALATIANS 5:1
It is for freedom that Christ has set us free. Stand firm, then, and do not let yourselves be burdened again by a yoke of slavery.

Accepting the responsibility of a disciplined life is accepting the responsibility of financial discipline. Accepting this financial responsibility will ultimately result in reducing major stress in our lives. It will give us unequaled freedom, the flexibility to come and go and live anywhere, and enormous personal fulfillment. I believe God wants us to have the freedom to respond to His call. This means we must be flexible and mobile in a relatively short time period. That is simply not possible when you live undisciplined financial lives. When we live from paycheck to paycheck and payment to payment, we simply do not have mobility.

God has given us dominion over the earth. But we have taken our God-given freedoms and submitted ourselves to the bondage of burdensome materialism. Instead of serving God, we live to serve our lenders. Instead of being free of our wants and desires and having a great testimony that God is taking care of our needs, we show our friends, family, and neighbors that we have a lack of trust and confidence in God's ability to care for us—so much so that we go into debt to get things He has not supplied.

Principle 18

The Principle of
MANAGING OUR POSSESSIONS

*W*hat a person does with personal possessions is important to God. Our life's stewardship should reflect God's interest in all that He has entrusted to us. Genesis 1:26 records that God made man to rule over all the earth and all life on earth, both plant and animal. In Genesis 2:15, man was made steward over the Garden, which housed gold, precious stones, and rivers. In other words, man was created for more than going to heaven after a lifetime of waiting. He was created to be a faithful steward over the work of God's hands. This is a great trust that God places in our lives. More than just money or finances, it is our entire life, which we must handle with faithfulness, responsibility, accountability, honesty, and integrity. Stewardship is bringing everything we have to offer under the lordship of Christ. What kind of a person makes a good steward? A person who has a great respect for God and His creation.

The manner in which we obtain, hold, and disburse our possessions and finances is of utmost importance to God. Jesus said in Luke 16:11, "If therefore ye have not been faithful in the unrighteous mammon, who will commit to your trust the true riches?" (KJV). Mammon means "gain" or "wealth."

What is so much better than money that God calls them "true riches"? True riches could be a lot of things, but certainly they include the gift of salvation, the gift of grace, the gift of mercy, and the gift of the Holy Spirit. The Scriptures present a wonderful reality. Second Peter 1:3 notes, "According as his divine power hath given unto us all things that pertain unto life and godliness" (KJV).

Accepting the responsibility of handling our possessions means we must be willing to place all we have at God's disposal. Not everyone is successful in this matter, even in biblical days, as is recorded in the following story:

MATTHEW 19:16–22
Now a man came up to Jesus and asked, "Teacher, what good thing must I do to get eternal life?" "Why do you ask me about what is good?" Jesus replied. "There is only One who is good. If you want to enter life, obey the commandments." "Which ones?" the man inquired. Jesus replied, "Do not murder, do not commit adultery, do not steal, do not give false testimony, honor your father and mother, and love your neighbor as yourself." "All these I have kept," the young man said. "What do I still lack?" Jesus answered, "If you want to be perfect, go, sell your possessions and give to the poor, and you will have treasure in heaven. Then come, follow me." When the young man heard this, he went away sad, because he had great wealth.

Wealth can keep us from inheriting the kingdom of heaven if it steals our hearts from their rightful place in God's hands. In the story of the rich young ruler, Jesus could see clearly what was lord in his life. He was willing to obey Jesus until it came to money, obviously the true ruler of his heart. God does not ask each of us to sell our possessions and give to the poor, as He did this man, but the principle is still true today. It is about a willing heart. When we are truly surrendered to God's will in our lives, we have a heart that is willing to give everything to God. When our hands are too busy grasping what God has given us, we are unable to receive more. Instead, we should live in such a way that we hold what God has given to us with open hands facing toward heaven. Such a posture says, "Whatever You've given me is Yours, Lord. I freely offer it." Notice though that when we offer, we are also in a position to receive.

To handle possessions well, we must have something for which to be responsible. To have something, we must have been receivers of something. Everything we have we received from someone else. Everything we have came from somewhere. Our automobiles, our home, our furniture, our money, our jobs—they all came from outside of us. Paul makes this point in 1 Corinthians 4:7: "For who makes you different from anyone else? What do you have that you did not receive? And if you did receive it, why do you boast as though you did not?"

Our responsibility to handle our possessions properly means understanding that as we have received with open hands we also give with open hands. Once in receipt of possessions, we don't respond by clenching our fists and holding tight all we have been given. This would indicate an abnormal love for things, making us self-centered, proud, and selfish. When we have been blessed with possessions, it becomes our responsibility to care for them and share them as the need arises.

If God can trust us with the least possessions, then He can trust us with great possessions. Once we have received, we cannot get anymore until we have proven responsible and able to handle what we have, whether it is money or other possessions. Once we are found faithful with little, we can create the capacity to handle more. When we have an open hand, God will fill it. If we close it to others, we close it to God. When we give away, we fill up again. This creates the cycle of stewardship. This is the way God intended for us to live.

> LUKE 16:10
> *"Whoever can be trusted with very little can also be trusted with much, and whoever is dishonest with very little will also be dishonest with much."*

God gives us things to extend His kingdom. They are kingdom property, and we have become mere caretakers. The possessions are entrusted to our management for but a temporary time period. God has given them to us for use in our ERA. No, that's not an Individual Retirement Account, but something much more significant—an Eternal Return Account. How we use these possessions is an indicator of how good we are as managers.

Have you reached your limit of responsibility, or can God trust you with more?

Principle 19

The Principle of MATERIALISM

PROVERBS 21:17
He who loves pleasure will become poor; whoever loves wine and oil will never be rich.

This verse tells us that loving pleasure and overindulgence squanders assets and prevents us from building proper financial resources.

Jesus said this in Luke 12:15: "Watch out! Be on your guard against all kinds of greed; a man's life does not consist in the abundance of his possessions."

In the United States, we live in a world filled with things and stuff. A life that revolves around things and stuff can be defined as a life filled with materialism. Too often, our spending habits are built upon the foundation of materialism because we want things and more things. We just can't seem to get enough stuff.

Now hear me out. Having things is not the problem. Having the money to be able to purchase things is not the problem, but stuff and things should not be bought just because you have the money. Of course, if you don't have the money, they should not even be considered. As biblical stewards, we are not to spend the Master's money on things we don't need. That would be very foolish.

So if having wealth is not the problem, and having possessions is not the problem, then what is the obstacle, the potential stumbling block? The spiritual problem comes with the love of things. When we can't get enough, when we must have more, this is where we stumble spiritually.

Many parents attempt to express their love for their children by overindulgence in gifts and money. Perhaps this is their way of making up for being absentee parents, workaholic parents, or for a lack of spiritual guidance in the family. But this contradicts many other biblical principles. The Christian way is all about servanthood and sacrifice, not materialism and overindulgence.

One definition of materialism is, "The tendency to give undue importance to material interests; devotion to the material nature and its wants" (The American Heritage® Dictionary of the English Language, Fourth Edition).

Another definition of materialism is, "A desire for wealth and material possessions with little interest in ethical or spiritual matters" (Webster's Revised Unabridged Dictionary, © 1996, 1998 MICRA, Inc.).

A. W. Tozer said, "Never own anything; get rid of the sense of possessing!"

R. C. Sproul said:
Materialism is a view of life that regards the possession of material things as the highest good, the summum bonum. It involves more than a mere appreciation of physical things. It goes beyond the simple enjoyment of material benefits. This view is both radical and an ism. It is radical because it makes material things the heart or "root" (radix) of all human happiness. It is an ism because it turns the neutral word "material" into a philosophy of life."

Here is a biblical story about a fool and his possessions. He was even called a fool by God!

LUKE 12:16–21
And he told them this parable: "The ground of a certain rich man produced a good crop. He thought to himself, What shall I do? I have no place to store my crops. Then he said, 'This is what I'll do. I will tear down my barns and build bigger ones, and there I will store all my grain and my goods. And I'll say to myself, You have plenty of good things laid up for many years. Take life easy; eat, drink and be merry.' But God said to him, 'You fool! This very night your life will be demanded from you. Then who will get what you have prepared for yourself?' This is how it will be with anyone who stores up things for himself but is not rich toward God."

Well, what do you think? Was he a fool? Not many people have been so singled out by God. But before you jump on the bandwagon in agreement, read the story again. This story seems to be a picture of the American Dream! The rich man was probably a hard and productive worker. He built and saved and toiled for a lifetime. This is not unlike some people today. They purchase their first little house, and when they outgrow it, they sell it and buy a bigger one. And when they get a little equity in the place, they put it on the market and look for a bigger, better, nicer, newer house!

The man in Luke 12 was shrewd. He was a builder; he was an investor. There is no evidence that he was dishonest, no evidence that he broke the law, and no evidence that he evaded paying taxes. None whatsoever. Some people today are just like him. They write bestselling books, give expensive seminars, have university buildings named after them, and are proclaimed publicly as entrepreneurs—the individuals that make America great! They work hard, invest well, and retire early.

Yet in Luke 12, God called this man a fool. Why? Is it wrong to be successful? Is it wrong to have wealth? Does this mean Christians should be poor? No! Abraham, Isaac, Jacob, Joseph, David, Solomon, Daniel, Joseph of Arimathea, and Cornelius were all wealthy. Some of them, in fact, were extremely wealthy.

So what's the difference between the man called a fool by God and these great Old Testament patriarchs and New Testament characters? The difference is this: This man's outlook on life was totally self-centered. Everything he did was for himself. Every event, every purchase, every sale, everything was all about his personal ease and happiness. In his mind, HE, not God, was the sole owner of his life and his possessions. And his priorities were so badly skewed that he deserved the tag "fool."

He used his wealth for himself rather than for the kingdom of God. His security was all wrapped up in his ability, his money, and his possessions. He was headed for a retirement life of ease, but one without God. A retirement of self-serving gratification, not a retirement of servanthood.

Yes, it's true that the Abrahams, Isaacs, Jacobs, Josephs, Davids, Solomons, and Daniels of the Bible were rich. But here is the difference between them and the Luke 12 fool: They had wealth, but each of them was totally devoted to God.

Is it wrong to enjoy the blessing of God? Of course not, but the blessing of God does mean we must have our priorities right in life. First, God must be recognized as the source of all things. Second, He must be credited with full ownership of all we possess. Third, it must be known that our spiritual prosperity is infinitely more important than our material prosperity.

> 3 JOHN 1:2
> *Beloved, I pray that you may prosper in all things and be in health, just as your soul prospers. (NKJV)*

> JOSHUA 1:8
> *Do not let this Book of the Law depart from your mouth; meditate on it day and night, so that you may be careful to do everything written in it. Then you will be prosperous and successful.*

Principle 20

The Principle of **PERSONAL DILIGENCE**

PROVERBS 21:25–26
The sluggard's craving will be the death of him, because his hands refuse to work. All day long he craves for more, but the righteous give without sparing.

ROMANS 12:11
Not slothful in business; fervent in spirit; serving the Lord. (KJV)

PROVERBS 24:30–34
I went past the field of the sluggard, past the vineyard of the man who lacks judgment; thorns had come up everywhere, the ground was covered with weeds, and the stone wall was in ruins. I applied my heart to what I observed and learned a lesson from what I saw: A little sleep, a little slumber, a little folding of the hands to rest—and poverty will come on you like a bandit and scarcity like an armed man.

$\mathcal{I}$t is everyone's responsibility to be hardworking, persistent, and diligent. The person who has no diligence is lazy—a sluggard, if you will. The sluggard...what can be said about this kind of person? Is he self-centered or lazy? Does he rest? Does he do what he wants to do without regard to others? Certainly all these things probably describe a sluggard, but much more could be said.

At the very least, a sluggard has a major problem with procrastination. His motto would be "Never do today what you can put off until tomorrow," always with good intentions, always just about ready to start a job—but not quite. The sluggard probably gets started on a few jobs, and with some of those tasks he may even get some things done, but he never quite gets them finished or brought to completion.

What is his excuse? Maybe he didn't have all the tools to finish the job. Maybe he wasn't feeling well. Maybe the rain was on its way, or it could just be that the sun wasn't shining brightly enough. Perhaps his excuse is that the job became bigger than he was expecting or it became more time-consuming than he was willing to commit to. Whatever the excuse, the sluggard always finds a reason for not finishing the job.

The sluggard as portrayed in Proverbs is an example of what not to be like and presents a valuable lesson for us. Proverbs 20:4 tells us that the sluggard is too lazy to pull a plow in the springtime and therefore has no harvest in the fall. In Proverbs 22:13, he lets his mind wander, but refuses to move his body. He has a great reason why he can't get it into gear. He says there could be a lion outside, and if he goes out to work, he could be murdered in the streets!

Whatever the situation, when the sluggard makes up his mind that he doesn't feel like working today, he will find an excuse to justify his inaction. He will find some kind of plausible explanation for his decision. He will leap to shirk his responsibilities, for he has a quick mind and a lazy body.

The ancient Chinese philosopher Confucius once said, "The expectations of life depend upon diligence; the mechanic that would perfect his work must first sharpen his tools."

Samuel Johnson noted, "If your determination is fixed, I do not counsel you to despair. Few things are impossible to diligence and skill. Great works are performed not by strength, but perseverance."

William Penn equated faith and diligence when he said, "Patience and diligence, like faith, remove mountains."

Proverbs 12:27 says, "The lazy man does not roast his game, but the diligent man prizes his possessions." Here is the picture of a sluggard who is not only lazy, but also wasteful. Not only does he do what he wants, when he wants, but he is also is a great waster of resources and provision. He goes out, hunts his game, and kills it. But after the fun of the hunt, the work never begins. He could prepare the provision for his family or the poor, the needy and the hungry, but he instead chooses to walk away from it—lets it die and lie and rot and does not make the food available for the hungry.

Diligent people don't waste God's provision. They thank God for it and prepare the meat for future use. They share it with others. They continue to diligently use the resources available to them.

Sluggards are not like that. They are not interested in saving re-sources and helping others. To them it is all about the fun of the sport. They are wasteful about everything. Sluggards proclaim that when their ships come in, they will begin to give. Herein lies the problem: If you never sent out your ship to begin with, you cannot expect it to come in. For what kind of ship are you waiting? Money does not fall from heaven. God does not give money miracles to a lazy, slothful person.

If you don't want to live the life of a sluggard, you need to get your act together. You need to start working and using godly wisdom and insight. You need to understand your calling and purpose in life and set out objectives that will allow you to live that fulfilled life. Then, and only then, will you reap with joy what you have sowed with tears.

Principle 21

The Principle of
PERSONAL PRODUCTIVITY

$\mathcal{G}$ood stewardship is not merely an occupation or a profession; rather it involves being productive. In Jesus' parable of the talents in Matthew 25, the stewards reported their earnings. One servant, however, merely hid his entrustment and earned no increase—he lost his portion. The faithful ones not only had increases, but also received more because of their faithfulness. From the very beginning, God commanded creation to be fruitful. God is energetic, creative, imaginative, and is the life giver. Stewards are also to be concerned with productivity and so cultivate God's creation to be productive.

It is wonderful to live in a productive society. Productive societies are composed of many productive individuals. When my days are full of productive tasks, I enjoy life. My normal going-to-sleep activity is to close my eyes and mentally survey all the things I accomplished during the day. If I have had an efficient and industrious day, I fall right to sleep.

A warning about being productive is seen in Jesus' story about the unfruitful branch of His kingdom, which He says will be cut off by the husbandman (John 15:1-5). God wants to have a productive kingdom and stewards who will be faithful.

As good stewards, we are required to work hard. If you work for someone else, you need to do it with everything you have. Give more than is required; go the second mile and the third and fourth. Proverbs 6:6-11 says:

> Go to the ant, you sluggard; consider its ways and be wise! It has no commander, no overseer or ruler, yet it stores its provisions in summer and gathers its food at harvest. How long will you lie there, you sluggard? When will you get up from your sleep? A little sleep, a little slumber, a little folding of the hands to rest and poverty will come on you like a bandit and scarcity like an armed man.

Check out the ant. The ant has no one to tell it what to do—no supervisor, no overseer, and yet it is a self-starter, a self-motivator. The ant works all summer long gathering food for the harvest season. This Scripture extends a wake-up call to the sluggard, hoping for some kind of response. It says to the sluggard, "Have you not slept enough?" "How long can you possibly sleep?" "Do you want to go hungry?" "Do you want to go through life looking for handouts because you have not the wherewithal to earn your own keep?"

Scriptures on Productivity

1 THESSALONIANS 4:11
> Make it your ambition to lead a quiet life, to mind your own business and to work with your hands, just as we told you, so that your daily life may win the respect of outsiders and so that you will not be dependent on anybody.

PROVERBS 22:29
Do you see a man skilled in his work? He will serve before kings; he will not serve before obscure men.

ECCLESIASTES 9:10
Whatever your hand finds to do, do it with all your might.

PROVERBS 20:4
A sluggard does not plow in season; so at harvest time he looks but finds nothing.

According to the above Scriptures, we should approach life and work like the ant. Although the ant has no boss, it still works extremely hard to provide for its needs. A lot of people today could learn a valuable lesson from the ant. Some today have the attitude, If I can get someone else to do the work for me, then why should I exert myself? Why not let someone else do the work? Why not let the government provide for me? Many today have little or no initiative, are not able to put themselves to work, and must always have someone else instruct them and supervise them in order to keep them working. The biblical way is for each person to accept the personal responsibility to be a contributor to society and a person of productivity.

Principle 22

The Principle of
PROPER USE OF MONEY

*I*s it wrong to have money? Does being spiritual mean you must give up all your possessions and live in poverty? Are possessions bad? Doesn't the Scripture say money is the root of all evil? Of course, the accurate and truthful answer to each of these questions is "no." The Bible does say in 1 Timothy 6:10 that the "love" of money is a root of all evil. God created the world. He created all the varied pleasures of life itself. 1 Timothy 4 lets us know that everything God created was good and that nothing is to be rejected when it is received with thanksgiving. Satan did not and cannot create anything. All he can do is attempt to corrupt every good thing God has given to us.

Mark 10 tells us the story of the rich young ruler. Here was a decent person, one who had worked hard and had become very wealthy. We are not told that he had any real problems with theft, murder, adultery, perjury, or anything else. In fact, he admitted to living by the Ten Commandments from a very young age. The rich young ruler wanted eternal or everlasting life. But when Jesus, the Everlasting Life, looked into his eyes and said to give all he had to the poor and follow Him, the cost seemed too high. Jesus said that by doing this, the young ruler would have treasure in heaven. But the young man went away sad.

What was the rich young ruler's situation? Was it that he had too much money and that people with great wealth cannot go to heaven? Of course not! His stumbling block was that his wealth had him. Possessions and money are not bad—in fact, they are good when used as tools to support the kingdom of God. The young man suffered from foolish decision making. When the greatest opportunity of his life was staring him in the face, he chose to reject it in favor of his money. He had not learned the principle of the proper use of money.

It is not all about having great wealth and using it the wrong way. Many Christians have very little money, yet have to overcome the same obstacle as the rich young ruler. When Jesus was warning the rich, He was not classifying people according to the amount of money they had. He was cautioning them about how attached they were to what they had. You can be overly attached to your money and possessions whether you have just a meager amount or great wealth. Will your money become your blessing or your curse? Can money buy happiness? Can it buy contentment? Can it buy peace of mind?

Contrast the man of wealth in Mark 10 with the founder of the Quaker Oats Company, who gave 70 percent of his income to God. Or contrast the Chicago Seven to

Abraham, the wealthy father of many nations. Abraham was not only a great man of faith, but also a very wealthy individual. Solomon was probably the richest man of his day. Barnabas, an early New Testament local church leader, was also wealthy but used his money and affluence to extend the kingdom of God.

James 5:1-3 speaks to the wealthy who use their money for personal gratification. James tells them that they will weep and howl because of all the misery that is coming upon them. He boldly says that their gold and silver is plagued and their precious metals will soon rust. James points out that it is foolish to value and esteem riches so highly that it causes corruption. It is harmless to possess riches, as long as the riches do not possess us.

Jesus recommends that we not stockpile our treasures in this life, at the expense of accumulating our treasures for the hereafter. In other words, it makes much more sense to accumulate wealth for the long haul in eternity. Time here on earth is the short haul—the temporary vapor of life. Life in eternity, life in heaven, is the long-term commitment.

You own nothing and God owns everything. Whatever you have, God allowed you to accumulate. But when you die, how much of your money will you leave behind? All of it! When you die, how much of your money will you take with you? None of it!

Ultimately, you own nothing. You won't take your new BMW with you. You won't take those diamond rings or precious jewelry with you. You won't take your house with you. You won't take any property with you. You won't take any of the possessions you have managed to accumulate here on earth. You won't take your body because you don't own it. When your spirit leaves your body, your body will return to dust.

Principle 23

The Principle of
REFUSING TO ACCEPT WORLD VIEWS

ROMANS 12:2
Don't copy the behavior and customs of this world, but be a new and different person with a fresh newness in all you do and think. Then you will learn from your own experience how his ways will really satisfy you. (RSV)

We must resist the world's view of wealth, happiness, and possessions. We do not have to have it all! Instead of trying to have it all, why not try to see how many needs you can meet in your giving stewardship?

Resisting the views of the world in handling our personal finances means we don't trust in riches, money, or possessions. These things will surely pass away. But we do trust in God. He is our sole provider and should be in control of our lives.

We live in a culture that continuously encourages us to buy, buy, buy. From billboards to television commercials, from radio advertisements to magazine ads, we are told about everything we don't have, but must have right away. It takes a lot of stamina just to resist accepting what society tries to impose upon our thinking. The Bible cautions us in these matters and encourages us to withstand such pressure.

Success and wealth look different from a Christian perspective. Wealth is having what you need. Wealth is more than money. Our society's worldview is to look for ways to make a lot of money, very quickly, by doing little work. A constant lookout for get-rich schemes is prevalent.

The biblical principle centers on productivity, hard work, personal diligence, and God's blessing. We are to use our God-given talents to partner with God's wisdom. If God chooses to bless us with wealth, then we properly use the riches God allows us to extend and further His kingdom.

Reject the worldview of materialism and self-centeredness at any cost. You won't benefit from having it all. If you have a family, trying to have it all will be a detriment to spiritual growth and may even cause major missteps in later years. Pray when tempted to jump at the latest scheme. If you have trouble resisting the constant bombardment of advertisements that make you want to go out and make an immediate purchase, shut off the television or turn down the radio.

There is another way: Be a good steward of God's gifts to you. Be careful what you do with your money, for someday you will have to account for how you used God's blessing. Every purchase you make should be a spiritual decision. After all, you are using His resources.

Principle 24

The Principle of RIGHTEOUS ATTITUDES

2 CORINTHIANS 9:6–9
Remember this: Whoever sows sparingly will also reap sparingly, and whoever sows generously will also reap generously. Each man should give what he has decided in his heart to give, not reluctantly or under compulsion, for God loves a cheerful giver. And God is able to make all grace abound to you, so that in all things at all times, having all that you need, you will abound in every good work.

The purpose in grouping this entire passage together is that there is a group message here. Commitment stands alone, but is insufficient without right attitudes. Giving freely and cheerfully is great, but insufficient in itself. There must be commitment. Overriding all is the unchangeable law of sowing and reaping. We get out what we put in. We harvest what we plant. The fruit is the same as our seed.

We must have a commitment to giving, and it must be settled in our hearts and minds once and for all. If God owns it all—and He does—then our maximum part is the 90 percent. Our attitude is to be one of happiness in returning the money to its rightful owner. We are happy to give to the very Giver of life. All that we have is His. When we give, we help further the work of His kingdom. And furthermore, when we give with commitment, right attitude, cheerfulness, and right motives, His grace abounds toward us in every good work. This means that we will have all that we need and more.

Principle 25

The Principle of RIGHTEOUS GIVING

PROVERBS 21:26
But the righteous give without sparing.

*T*his personal story is told by Eddie Ogan. It illustrates this principle of giving without sparing.

I'll never forget Easter 1946. I was fourteen, my little sister Ocy was twelve, and my older sister Darlene sixteen. We lived at home with our mother, and the four of us knew what it was to do without many things. My dad had died five years before, leaving Mom with seven school kids to raise and no money.

By 1946 my older sisters were married, and my brothers had left home. A month before Easter, the pastor of our church announced that a special Easter offering would be taken to help a poor family. He asked everyone to save and give sacrificially. When we got home, we talked about what we could do. We decided to buy 50 pounds of potatoes and live on them for a month. This would allow us to save twenty dollars of our grocery money for the offering. When we thought that if we kept our electric lights turned out as much as possible and didn't listen to the radio, we'd save money on that month's electric bill.

Darlene got as many house and yard cleaning jobs as possible, and both of us babysat for everyone we could. For fifteen cents we could buy enough cotton loops to make three pot holders to sell for a dollar. We made twenty dollars on pot holders. That month was one of the best of our lives. Every day we counted the money to see how much we had saved. At night we'd sit in the dark and talk about how the poor family was going to enjoy having the money the church would give them.

We had about eighty people in church, so figured that whatever amount of money we had to give, the offering would surely be twenty times that much. After all, every Sunday the pastor had reminded everyone to save for the sacrificial offering.

The day before Easter, Ocy and I walked to the grocery store and got the manager to give us three crisp twenty-dollar bills and one ten-dollar bill for all our change. We ran all the way home to show Mom and Darlene. We had never had so much money before.

That night we were so excited we could hardly sleep. We didn't care that we wouldn't have new clothes for Easter; we had seventy for the sacrificial offering. We could hardly wait to get to church! On Sunday morning, rain was pouring. We didn't own an umbrella, and the church was over a mile from our home, but it didn't seem to matter how wet we got. Darlene had cardboard in her shoes to fill the holes. The cardboard came apart, and her feet got wet.

But we sat in church proudly. I heard some teenagers talking about the Smith girls having on their old dresses. I looked at them in their new clothes, and I felt rich. When the sacrificial offering was taken, we were sitting on the second row from the front. Mom put in the ten-dollar bill, and each of us kids put in twenty dollars. As we walked home after church, we sang all the way. At lunch, Mom had a surprise for us. She had bought a dozen eggs, and we had boiled Easter eggs with our fried potatoes!

Late that afternoon the minister drove up in his car. Mom went to the door, talked with him for a moment, and then came back with an envelope in her hand. We asked what it was, but she didn't say a word. She opened the envelope, and out fell a bunch of money. There were three crisp twenty-dollar bills, one ten-dollar bill and seventeen dollar bills.

Mom put the money back in the envelope. We didn't talk, just sat and stared at the floor. We had gone from feeling like millionaires to feeling like poor white trash. We kids had such a happy life that we felt sorry for anyone who didn't have our Mom and Dad for parents and a house full of brothers and sisters and other kids visiting constantly. We thought it was fun to share silverware and see whether we got the spoon or the fork that night. We had two knives that we passed around to whoever needed them. I knew we didn't have a lot of things other people had, but I'd never thought we were poor.

That Easter day I found out we were. The minister had brought us the money for the poor family, so we must be poor. I didn't like being poor. I looked at my dress and worn-out shoes and felt so ashamed—I didn't even want to go back to church. Everyone there probably already knew we were poor! I thought about school. I was in the ninth grade and at the top of my class of over a hundred students. I wondered if the kids at school knew that we were poor. I decided that I could quit school since I had finished the eighth grade. That was all the law required at that time. We sat in silence for a long time. Then it got dark, and we went to bed. All that week, we girls went to school and came home, and no one talked much.

Finally on Saturday, Mom asked us what we wanted to do with the money. What did poor people do with money? We didn't know. We'd never known we were poor. We didn't want to go to church on Sunday, but Mom said we had to. Although it was a sunny day, we didn't talk on the way. Mom started to sing, but no one joined in, and she only sang one verse. At church we had a missionary speaker. He talked about how churches in Africa made buildings out of sun dried bricks, but they needed money to buy roofs. He said one hundred would put a roof on a church. The minister said, "Can't we all sacrifice to help these poor people?" We looked at each other and smiled for the first time in a week. Mom reached into her purse and pulled out the envelope. She passed it to Darlene. Darlene gave it to me, and I handed it to Ocy. Ocy put it in the offering.

When the offering was counted, the minister announced that it was a little over a hundred dollars. The missionary was excited. He hadn't expected such a large offering from our small church. He said, "You must have some rich people in this church." Suddenly it struck us! We had given eighty-seven dollars of that "little over a hundred dollars." We were the rich family in the church! Hadn't the missionary said so? From that day on I've never been poor again. I've always remembered how rich I am because I have Jesus!

Principle 26

The Principle of
RIGHTEOUS RELATIONSHIPS

MATTHEW 5:23–24
Therefore, if you are offering your gift at the altar and there remember that your brother has something against you, leave your gift there in front of the altar. First go and be reconciled to your brother; then come and offer your gift.

According to people in the ski boat industry, no one has a history that can compare to that of Correct Craft. Correct Craft invented ski boats and has been building them nearly as long as waterskiing itself has existed. When you talk about Correct Craft, you are talking about the Meloon family. For seventy-nine years, the Correct Craft family has been dedicated to providing customers with the finest inboard boats available. Located in Florida, some of the finest watercraft come from their factory.

The U.S. Coast Guard, under the direction of George Washington, was organized by a Meloon ancestor. The Meloon brothers were in the family business together. Correct Craft, previously named the Pine Castle Boat and Construction

Company, is a pleasure boat manufacturing company that was owned and operated by Ralph and Walter Meloon.

The year was 1945 and General Dwight D. Eisenhower needed to transport his troops located in Germany across the Rhine River. The government contracted with Correct Craft to build three hundred boats in just thirty days. The company went into action, hiring an additional 250 workers. Shutting down local streets for manufacturing purposes and moving much of the production outside, they completed the job with some four days to spare. According to military experts, because Correct Craft was able to produce that many boats in a short time, some fifteen thousand military lives were saved. The company was awarded the Army and Navy's prestigious "E" award, and this accounting of what happened is a piece of American history recorded in the National Archives in Washington, D.C.

During the Korean conflict, the government once again was at their doorstep and ordered three thousand boats. But a sad thing happened this time—because a government inspector was looking for bribes, many of the boats were rejected for not being up to the proper specifications. Over six hundred of the boats had to be shelved. The result was the company going into bankruptcy mode and filing for Chapter 11 protection. The company reduced its workforce from five hundred to twenty-five persons.

At the end of filing in 1965, the Meloons made a personal commitment to seek out all their creditors (whom they owed nothing to legally) and paid them in full. Even though the court had already cancelled 80 percent of their debt, over the course of eighteen years, the company still tracked down 228 creditors and paid the already-forgiven debt. No only did they repay their debt, but they also forgave the inspector for his role in seeking company bribes.

Righteous relationships do matter, whether it be personal or business relationships. By operating with biblical principles, the company has since grown to be a very successful, award-winning company.

Principle 27

The Principle of
SEEKING RIGHTEOUSNESS FIRST

MATTHEW 6:33
"But seek first His kingdom and His righteousness, and all these things will be given to you as well."

*P*utting God first in our lives relieves us from the task of having to worry about everything else. Seeking His kingdom and righteousness first is simply making God the priority in our lives. There is always the temptation to put your money first. Do you remember the rich young ruler who came to Jesus and said that he wanted to follow Christ? Jesus' response didn't make him real happy. Jesus told him to give his money away and follow Him. It wasn't the money that was wrong; it was that this young man placed his money ahead of and above all else.

If we have too much money, there is always the danger that we can depend upon it above all else.

Does your life reveal your desire to put God first? The Lord admonishes us to seek first His Kingdom, His way of doing things. We must ask God to help us develop an attitude of serving Him faithfully and a lifestyle that is free of debt and worry.

Principle 28

The Principle of
TIME STEWARDSHIP

$\mathcal{G}$od blesses individual effort. Receiving supernatural provision requires efficient and productive use of our time. We are required to redeem the minutes and capture the hours. We should be filling efficient days and occupying industrious weeks. Our effective and productive months should result in progressive years. We have a responsibility not to waste the precious little time we have been given.

Several years ago, I traveled to a small town with a couple of friends. Our mission was to paint the house of a dying man. The house was in need of a fresh coat of paint, and we were wanting to pay him a visit. Instead of just standing around watching his pain, we intended to help brighten his day by painting the house.

As we were saying our good-byes at the end of the day, he made a profound statement I still remember as if it were yesterday. He said, "It pays to give it all you've got

99

while you're on stage, because you never know when your act is up." Soon afterward, he died of cancer.

Time is our tool. It is a wonderful gift. We should not be a slave to it; we should put it to proper use as an investment for the future.

God is the giver of life and the giver of time. He has the right to expect us to use it wisely. We have a responsibility to make the most of it. Good stewards of time and finance are not only faithful and responsible, but also have an honesty and financial integrity about them.

God is the God of the past, present and future. He has no time constraints. He is not bound by the limitations of time. Time means nothing to Him. See what the Word says about it.

> 2 PETER 3:8
> *But do not forget this one thing, dear friends: With the Lord a day is like a thousand years, and a thousand years are like a day.*

On earth, we (you and I) are constrained by time. Our lives are but a few years at best. Our time is limited. Time means a lot to us. God has allotted us just a limited amount of years and, therefore, is very concerned about how wisely we spend those years.

> JOB 14:1–2
> *Man born of woman is of few days and full of trouble. He springs up like a flower and withers away; like a fleeting shadow, he does not endure.*

> PSALM 90:10
> *The length of our days is seventy years—or eighty, if we have the strength; yet their span is but trouble and sorrow, for they quickly pass, and we fly away.*

EPHESIANS 5:15–16
Be very careful, then, how you live—not as unwise but as wise, making the most of every opportunity, because the days are evil.

JOHN 9:4–5
"As long as it is day, we must do the work of him who sent me. Night is coming, when no one can work. While I am in the world, I am the light of the world."

Time is valuable and utterly irretrievable; it is a priceless commodity. Suppose your bank credited your account each morning with $86,400.00, carried no balance from day to day, and allowed you to keep no cash in your account. Then suppose every evening the bank canceled whatever you failed to use during the day.

We all have this kind of bank; its name is time. Every morning it credits us with 86,400 seconds. Every night it considers lost whatever time we have failed to invest for good during the day. It carries over no balance. It allows no overdrafts. Each day it opens up a new account. Each night it burns the records of the day. If you failed to use the day's deposits, the loss is yours.

We are all given 1,440 minutes each day, 168 hours each week. This makes fifty-two weeks each year for which we must account. In spite of its value and unique characteristics, we probably waste time more thoughtlessly than anything else.

Adlai Stevenson once said, "It's not the days in your life, but the life in your days." In other words, it's not how much you do that counts; it's how much you get done that has purpose and lasting benefit.

101

This seems to be the great paradox in life. We generally feel as though we don't have enough time, yet we have all the time there is. Time is not the problem; the problem is how we use our allotted time.

Principle 29

The Principle of
UNDERSTANDING HARD WORK

$\mathcal{G}$od's supernatural provision does not replace hard work and persistent labor. Working and doing our part is never an easy task. It is rewarding, but challenging. Only God has the power to speak the word and cause something to happen instantly, but with man, work is necessary to accomplish an end result. In the book of Genesis, Adam was the sole steward appointed over all natural resources, as well as plant and animal life—a substantial entrustment from God. So when Adam disobeyed and lost that leadership, it affected a lot more than his descendants; it affected the sea, the air, the earth, and life as well.

When the steward (Adam) went astray, that which had been entrusted to him was severely injured. According to Romans 8:22, the whole earth groans in travail. When Adam and Eve sinned, God judged them. Humans were required to leave the plush Garden of Eden. God commanded in Genesis 3:19, "In the sweat of thy face shalt thou eat bread, till thou return unto the ground" (KJV).

Robert Ingersoll once said, "Every man is dishonest who lives upon the labor of others, no matter if he occupies a throne." The famous poet Robert Frost once gave an insightful quotation regarding work and people. He said, "The world is filled with willing people. Some willing to work, and the rest willing to let them."

In the United States, unlike Third World countries, we do not have a lower class. Though many think otherwise, all healthy people who want to work can do so, provide for themselves, have plenty to eat, and shelter for sleep. There are, of course, economic cycles of employment, job availability, discomfort, and times when growth opportunity is limited. When compared to the poor of this world, however, those who lack the most in this country are far better off than almost anyone anywhere else in the world.

In the Western world, a great deal of emphasis is placed upon having fun, spending time in leisurely activity, and taking care of the whims of "me." Many are content to put as little into their work as they think they can get away with. Far too many employees are receiving a full paycheck for less than a full day's work. Scriptures note in 2 Thessalonians 3:10, "If any would not work, neither should he eat" (KJV).

One sure sign of progress in your journey to enjoying all of God's benefits is simple recognition and understanding that there is no easy solution to a difficult challenge. While others are looking for their ship to come in or an easy path, you are quietly affirming to put your hand to the plow.

Principle 30

The Principle of WASTING NOTHING

JOHN 6:11–13
Jesus then took the loaves, gave thanks, and distributed to those who were seated as much as they wanted. He did the same with the fish. When they had all had enough to eat, he said to his disciples, "Gather the pieces that are left over. Let nothing be wasted." So they gathered them and filled twelve baskets with the pieces of the five barley loaves left over by those who had eaten.

In the story of the feeding of the five thousand, Christ recognized the need of the crowd of people. Knowing that the people were hungry and should be fed, He took stock of the available resources. All they could find was a lad with five loaves and two fishes. So Christ used that. Through the miracle of multiplication, the entire multitude was fed. Instead of resting in the praise of the contented participants, Jesus was very concerned that nothing be wasted.

Have you ever wasted the blessing of God? What has God provided miraculously for you that you squandered? What income and finances has He given to you that you let slip away with frivolous spending?

Many people, deep in debt and lacking in self-discipline in their spending and contentment level, complain that their employers don't pay them enough, their taxes are much too high, their business costs have skyrocketed, or render some other excuse why they cannot plan for their financial future. Of course, some of these excuses may have a certain amount of legitimacy to them, but they don't excuse a person from the responsibility of "no waste." The problem is not a lack of money; it is a lack of money management.

In Luke 16, the story is told of a dishonest steward who wasted his lord's goods, for which he was liable and was judged by his master.

In times past, I thought this steward was expelled from his job because of fraud. But the verses do not say this. If it were fraud, the master never would have let him stay around long enough to make alternate arrangements with the master's debtors. The verses simply infer that he was a bad money manager. If the steward had not been so fiscally challenged, the master could have had a better return on his investments, and not wasted the investment return he never received.

Today, we also are responsible to our Master for His creation and blessing. The scope of the parable suggests to us that it is important to manage our possessions and life on earth in such a way that will benefit us in eternal life. It's not that eternal life is our sole reason for managing our possessions judiciously. We should do this from our obedience, appreciation, and love for God.

We are wrong to make bad decisions by wasting the finances God has allowed to flow through our lives. All of us are stewards of what has been entrusted to us. We have a fiduciary responsibility to employ our wealth in acts of charity and good works, seeking an eternal return much the same way the dishonest steward employed his abilities to achieve the greatest temporal profit.

A lot of wasteful spending is incurred on perfectly good purchases, but more often than not, many purchases are for things we neither need nor use. How many attics, basements, and garages are full of great buys that were never used? If they were used, maybe they were rarely used. I could tell you about some exercise equipment I purchased that falls into this category. When all is said and done, the amount spent on these items, although seemingly legit, was very wasteful.

In Luke 16, the steward's lord commended him because he finally showed some ingenuity and ambition, even though it was for his own personal gain and benefit. The steward is not commended because he showed good credible sensitivity, but because he had done wisely for himself. The steward who was about to be dismissed made every attempt to better his cause through any means available—even though that cause was self-serving.

Most people today live far above and beyond their means. Their spending exceeds their earnings. Many people earn large incomes, but because of wasteful spending habits, little goes to personal investment, debt reduction, or charitable contribution.

By not spending wisely, or watching every dime spent and knowing for what it was spent, you will be led to poor financial decisions. Bad money management leads to a lot of personal and needless debt, and a lot of debt usually causes a tremendous amount of strain and anxiety on an otherwise good marriage. This kind of pressure can lead to anger, fighting, and possibly even divorce.

God is well able to meet your needs and offer supernatural provision, however there are personal disciplines you must apply before your hand is out and your heart is asking. There is a spiritual alignment that must be in order in your life.

Summary

$\mathcal{G}$od is interested in our willingness to manage and administrate all that He has given to us. In this sense, we could say that Jesus Christ is to be given complete freedom and lordship over our entire life. Like every other area of stewardship, God is interested in the whole picture, not just a part or a percentage.

The areas of good stewardship that He requires of us are almost limitless. They would of course include life itself, the gift of children, and the stewardship of His creation. Additionally, we would include the stewardship of our communication, the stewardship of time, the stewardship of truth, and the stewardship of talents or giftings. Discovering and developing our spiritual gifts and natural talents for the purpose of blessing others and glorifying God is our duty.

Nothing will be thrown into our laps. No, financial prosperity is not an unconditional providential blessing, and yes, conditions are attached. We are to take action and be proactive. The abilities and giftings God provides motivate us to action. Sometimes it takes our persistence in doing the same things faithfully with the heart of a servant. Other times it is time to try new things, new methods, and seek new opportunities. Sometimes the steady plodding brings the success of the blessed life.

Being a good steward begins with the blessing of God, but the test and fruit of good stewardship is how we use those blessings. Are we a conduit or do we stop the stream of God's favor. Do we allow the river to flow, or do we dam up God's supply? To me it is a matter of management, not ownership. Are we to give only a little and hoard the rest for our own pleasure? I think not. God expects us to use what we need (He has promised to supply our need), then to multiply and return the rest. Stewardship is trust, knowing and disbursing His blessing.

Source Material

21 Unbreakable Laws of Success, Max Anders, Thomas Nelson, 1996

A Christian Guide to Prosperity; Fries & Taylor, California: Communications Research, 1984

A Look At Stewardship, Word Aflame Publications, 2001

American Savings Education Council (http://www.asec.org)

Anointed For Business, Ed Silvoso, Regal, 2002

Avoiding Common Financial Mistakes, Ron Blue, Navpress, 1991

Baker Encyclopedia of the Bible; Walter Elwell, Michigan: Baker Book House, 1988

Becoming The Best, Barry Popplewell, England: Gower Publishing Company Limited, 1988

Business Proverbs, Steve Marr, Fleming H. Revell, 2001

Cheapskate Monthly, Mary Hunt

Commentary on the Old Testament; Keil-Delitzsch, Michigan: Eerdmans Publishing, 1986

Crown Financial Ministries, various publications

Customers As Partners, Chip Bell, Texas: Berrett-Koehler Publishers, 1994

Cut Your Bills in Half; Pennsylvania: Rodale Press, Inc., 1989

Debt-Free Living, Larry Burkett, Dimensions, 2001

Die Broke, Stephen M. Pollan & Mark Levine, HarperBusiness, 1997

Double Your Profits, Bob Fifer, Virginia: Lincoln Hall Press, 1993

Eerdmans' Handbook to the Bible, Michigan: William B. Eerdmans Publishing Company, 1987

Eight Steps to Seven Figures, Charles B. Carlson, Double Day, 2000

Everyday Life in Bible Times; Washington DC: National Geographic Society, 1967

Financial Dominion, Norvel Hayes, Harrison House, 1986

Financial Freedom, Larry Burkett, Moody Press, 1991

Financial Freedom, Patrick Clements, VMI Publishers, 2003

Financial Peace, Dave Ramsey, Viking Press, 2003

Financial Self-Defense; Charles Givens, New York: Simon And Schuster, 1990

Flood Stage, Oral Roberts, 1981

Generous Living, Ron Blue, Zondervan, 1997

Get It All Done, Tony and Robbie Fanning, New York: Pennsylvania: Chilton Book, 1979

Getting Out of Debt, Howard Dayton, Tyndale House, 1986

Getting Out of Debt, Mary Stephenson, Fact Sheet 436, University of Maryland Cooperative Extension Service, 1988

Giving and Tithing, Larry Burkett, Moody Press, 1991

God's Plan For Giving, John MacArthur, Jr., Moody Press, 1985

God's Will is Prosperity, Gloria Copeland, Harrison House, 1978

Great People of the Bible and How They Lived; New York: Reader's Digest, 1974

How Others Can Help You Get Out of Debt; Esther M. Maddux, Circular 759-3,

How To Make A Business Plan That Works, Henderson, North Island Sound Limited, 1989

How To Manage Your Money, Larry Burkett, Moody Press, 1999

How to Personally Profit From the Laws of Success, Sterling Sill, NIFP, Inc., 1978

How to Plan for Your Retirement; New York: Corrigan & Kaufman, Longmeadow Press, 1985

Is God Your Source?, Oral Roberts, 1992

It's Not Luck, Eliyahu Goldratt, Great Barrington, MA: The North River Press, 1994

Jesus CEO, Laurie Beth Jones, Hyperion, 1995

John Avanzini Answers Your Questions About Biblical Economics, Harrison House, 1992

Living on Less and Liking It More, Maxine Hancock, Chicago, Illinois: Moody Press, 1976

Making It Happen; Charles Conn, New Jersey: Fleming H. Revell Company, 1981

Master Your Money Or It Will Master You, Arlo E.
    Moehlenpah, Doing Good Ministries, 1999

Master Your Money; Ron Blue, Tennessee: Thomas Nelson,
    Inc. 1986

Miracle of Seed Faith, Oral Roberts, 1970

Mississippi State University Extension Service

Money, Possessions, and Eternity, Randy Alcorn, Tyndale
    House, 2003

More Than Enough, David Ramsey, Penguin Putnam Inc,
    2002

Moving the Hand of God, John Avanzini, Harrison House,
    1990

Multiplication, Tommy Barnett, Creation House, 1997

NebFacts, Nebraska Cooperative Extension

New York Post

One Up On Wall Street; New York: Peter Lynch, Simon And
    Schuster, 1989

Personal Finances, Larry Burkett, Moody Press, 1991

Portable MBA in Finance and Accounting; Livingstone,
    Canada: John Wiley & Sons, Inc., 1992

Principle-Centered Leadership, Stephen R. Covey, New
    York: Summit Books, 1991

Principles of Financial Management, Kolb & DeMong, Texas:
    Business Publications, Inc., 1988

Rapid Debt Reduction Strategies, John Avanzini, HIS
    Publishing, 1990

Real Wealth, Wade Cook, Arizona: Regency Books, 1985

See You At The Top, Zig Ziglar, Louisianna: Pelican Publishing Company, 1977

Seed-Faith Commentary on the Holy Bible, Oral Roberts, Pinoak Publications, 1975

Sharkproof, Harvey Mackay, New York: HarperCollins Publishers, 1993

Smart Money, Ken and Daria Dolan, New York: Random House, Inc., 1988

Strong's Concordance, Tennessee: Crusade Bible Publishers, Inc.,

Success by Design, Peter Hirsch, Bethany House, 2002

Success is the Quality of your Journey, Jennifer James, New York: Newmarket Press, 1983

Swim with the Sharks Without Being Eaten Alive, Harvey Mackay, William Morrow , 1988

The Almighty and the Dollar; Jim McKeever, Oregon: Omega Publications, 1981

The Challenge, Robert Allen, New York: Simon And Schuster, 1987

The Family Financial Workbook, Larry Burkett, Moody Press, 2002

The Management Methods of Jesus, Bob Briner, Thomas Nelson, 1996

The Millionaire Next Door, Thomas Stanley & William Danko, Pocket Books, 1996

The Money Book for Kids, Nancy Burgeson, Troll
Associates,1992

The Money Book for King's Kids; Harold E. Hill, New Jersey:
Fleming H. Revell Company, 1984

The Seven Habits of Highly Effective People, Stephen
Covey, New York: Simon And Schuster, 1989

The Wealthy Barber, David Chilton, California: Prima
Publishing, 1991

Theological Wordbook of the Old Testament, Chicago,
Illinois: Moody Press, 1981

Treasury of Courage and Confidence, Norman Vincent Peale,
New York: Doubleday & Co., 1970

True Prosperity, Dick Iverson, Bible Temple Publishing, 1993

Trust God For Your Finances, Jack Hartman, Lamplight
Publications, 1983

University of Georgia Cooperative Extension Service, 1985

Virginia Cooperative Extension

Webster's Unabridged Dictionary, Dorset & Baber, 1983

What Is an Entrepreneur; David Robinson, MA: Kogan Page
Limited, 1990

Word Meanings in the New Testament, Ralph Earle,
Michigan: Baker Book House, 1986

Word Pictures in the New Testament; Robertson, Michigan:
Baker Book House, 1930

Word Studies in the New Testament; Vincent, New York:
Charles Scribner's Sons, 1914

Worth

You Can Be Financially Free, George Fooshee, Jr., 1976, Fleming H. Revell Company.

Your Key to God's Bank, Rex Humbard, 1977

Your Money Counts, Howard, Dayton, Tyndale House, 1997

Your Money Management, MaryAnn Paynter, Circular 1271, University of Illinois Cooperative Extension Service, 1987.

Your Money Matters, Malcolm MacGregor, Bethany Fellowship, Inc., 1977

Your Road to Recovery, Oral Roberts, Oliver Nelson, 1986

Comment On Sources

Over the years I have collected bits and pieces of interesting material, written notes on sermons I've heard, jotted down comments on financial articles I've read, and gathered a lot of great information. It is unfortunate that I didn't record the sources of all of these notes in my earlier years. I gratefully extend my appreciation to the many writers, authors, teachers and pastors from whose articles and sermons I have gleaned much insight.

Rich Brott

Online Resources

American Savings Education Council (http://www.asec.org)

Bloomberg.com (http://www.bloomberg.com)

Bureau of the Public Debt Online (http://www.publicdebt. treas.gov)

BusinessWeek (http://www.businessweek.com)

Charles Schwab & Co., Inc. (http://www.schwab.com)

Consumer Federation of America (http://www. consumerfed.org)

Debt Advice.org (http://www.debtadvice.org)

Federal Reserve System (http://www.federalreserve.gov)

Fidelity Investments (http://www.fidelity.com)

Financial Planning Association (http://www.fpanet.org)

Forbes (www.forbes.com)

Fortune Magazine (http://www.fortune.com)

Generous Giving (http://www.generousgiving.org/)

Investing for Your Future (http://www.investing.rutgers. edu)

Kiplinger Magazine (http://www.kiplinger.com/)

Money Magazine (http://money.cnn.com)

MorningStar (http://www.morningstar.com)

MSN Money (http://moneycentral.msn.com)

Muriel Siebert (http://www.siebertnet.com)

National Center on Education and the Economy
(http://www.ncee.org)

National Foundation for Credit Counseling
(http://www.nfcc.org)

Quicken (http://www.quicken.com)

Smart Money (http://www.smartmoney.com)

Social Security Online (http://www.ssa.gov)

Standard & Poor's (http://www2.standardandpoors.com)

The Dollar Stretcher, Gary Foreman,
(http://www.stretcher.com)

The Vanguard Group (http://flagship.vanguard.com)

U.S. Securities and Exchange Commission
(http://www.sec.gov)

Yahoo! Finance (http://finance.yahoo.com)

Magazine Resources

Business Week

Consumer Reports

Forbes

Kiplinger's Personal Finance

Money

Smart Money

US News and World Report

Newspaper Resources

Barrons

Investors Business Daily

USA Today

Wall Street Journal

Washington Times

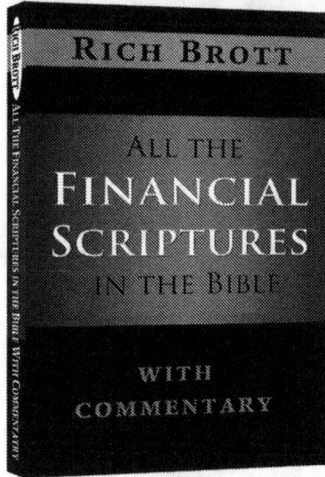

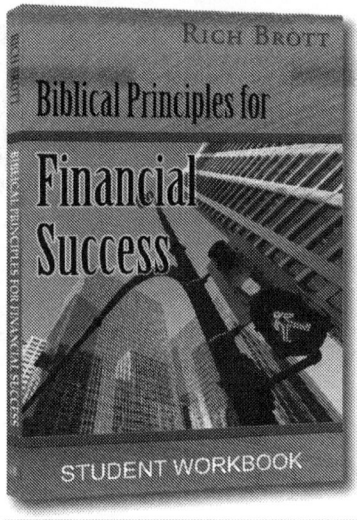

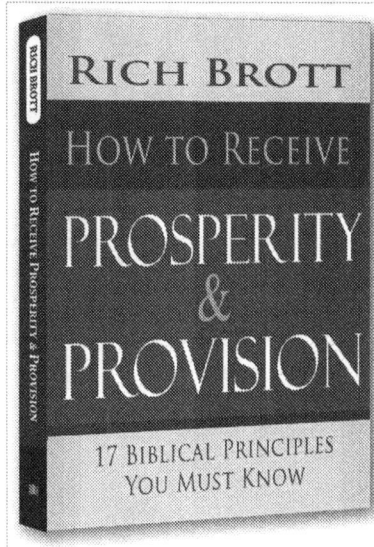

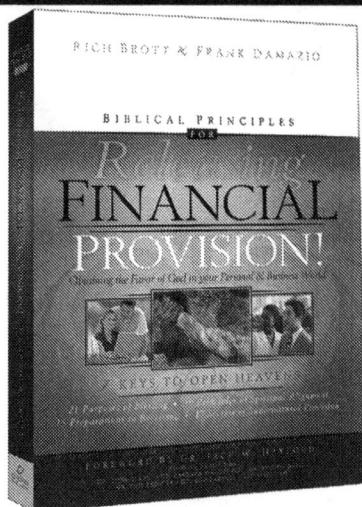

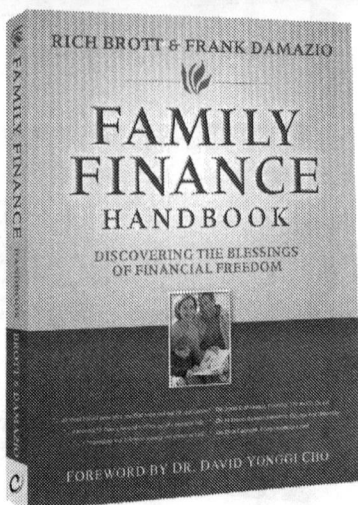

Additional Resources *by Rich Brott*

www.RichBrott.com

Also look for these new titles:

A Biblical Perspective on Giving Generously

A Biblical Perspective on Tithing Faithfully

abc
Book Publishing

Order online at:
www.RichBrott.com
www.amazon.com
www.barnesandnoble.com
www.booksamillion.com
www.citychristianpublishing.com
www.bordersstores.com

www.AbcBookPublishing.com

www.ingramcontent.com/pod-product-compliance
Lightning Source LLC
Chambersburg PA
CBHW071904200326
41519CB00016B/4505